This is a Parragon Book.

© Parragon 1997.

Parragon
13-17 Avonbridge Trading Estate
Atlantic Road, Avonmouth
Bristol, BS11 9QD

Produced by The Templar Company plc,
Pippbrook Mill, London Road, Dorking,
Surrey RH4 1JE

Written by Robert Snedden
Series Designer Mark Summersby
All photographs reproduced by permission of the Director, British
Geological Survey. ©NERC. and all photos by T. S. Bain, British
Geological Survey except for those on pages 40, 57, 58, 59,
74, 75, 83, 84 and the cover, which are copyright © The Natural
History Museum, London.

Particular thanks are extended to the Mineralogy & Petrology
Group, BGS Keyworth, and to the Photography Section, BGS
Edinburgh. The British Geological Survey possesses a large,
important, UK-wide collection of photographs of rocks, fossils,
minerals, mining and geologically related landscape features.
Photographic materials date from the early 1900s to the present
day. Selected recent materials can be accessed via the World Wide
Web @ http://www.nkw.ac.uk/bgs/

ISBN 0 7525 1664 7

·ROCKS &·
FOSSILS

·PARRAGON·

CONTENTS

INTRODUCTION

Rocks are divided into three major groups, according to the way in which they are formed.

Igneous rocks form from hot magma, or molten rock, rising up from deep inside the Earth to cooler regions where the magma solidifies. Volcanic igneous rocks are those that cool on the surface. The rapid cooling results in rocks such as basalts, which have fine crystals, or in glassy rocks, such as obsidian. Plutonic igneous rocks cool under the surface, where slow cooling results in coarse-grained rocks, such as granite, with larger crystals.

Sedimentary rocks, such as sandstone and mudstone, are formed from accumulated deposits of the weathered and eroded remains of older rocks, or from the remains of living things, such as the shells of marine organisms that make up some limestones, or the plant material that formed coal. Water, wind or ice deposit layer upon layer of fragments of rock as sediments. These sediments, often deposited in lakes or in the sea, can be several kilometres thick. The combination of the pressure from the weight of such a large mass and the action of water filtering through the sediments cements the fragments together to form rock. The process takes several million years to complete.

Metamorphic rocks are igneous rocks or sedimentary rocks that have been changed in character by high temperatures and possibly also high pressures, but without the rock actually melting. Thermal metamorphism is caused by molten magma rising into a crack in the Earth's crust and baking the rocks around it. Limestone is changed into marble in this way. Regional metamorphism is caused by the heat and high pressures brought about by large-scale movements of the crust, such as occurs in areas where mountain building is taking place. Shale is turned into slate by this process.

Rocks are what make up the Earth's crust, its outermost layer. The crust itself can be divided into two distinct types. The oceanic crust is made up of a layer of basalt and a layer of gabbro and similar rocks. The continental crust is composed largely of granite-type rocks. The rocks that make up the oceanic crust are relatively young, none being more than about 200 million years old. The oldest rocks of the continental crust are over 3 billion years old.

Fossils are the remains of animals or plants that have been preserved in rock. Generally only the hard parts of the organism, such as wood, teeth and bones are fossilised. In most fossils the organic remains are turned to stone, usually either by dissolved minerals filling the cavities in the organism, or by the minerals actually replacing the original organic material. The ideal conditions for fossil formation occur where sediments have been formed rapidly. This is why most fossils are found in sedimentary rock.

GRANITE

Granite is a coarse-grained igneous rock that is mainly composed of the minerals quartz, feldspar and mica. Sometimes crystals of these minerals may be found in cavities in the granite. Granite is most commonly found in varying shades and combinations of white, grey, pink and red, depending on the proportions of the various minerals that make it up. Formed deep within the Earth, granite is a hard-wearing rock and, when a granite outcrop reaches the surface, it is very resistant to weathering and erosion. The highest mountains in Britain are largely formed of granite, as are many moorland areas. Because of its hard-wearing characteristics, granite is frequently used as a building material.

GRANODIORITE

Granodiorite is a coarse-grained igneous rock that is most commonly grey-white in appearance, although there is also a pink and white form. It is found in the same places as granite and is also formed deep within the Earth. It is pushed up to the surface in mountainous regions. At the surface it may appear in dykes, vertical sheets of rock formed from cooled magma. Like granite, granodiorite is resistant to weathering and erosion and will often form part of rocky outcrops. This is one of the most common of the rocks in the granite family. There is less feldspar in granodiorite than there is in granite. The grains that make up the rock are roughly equal in size.

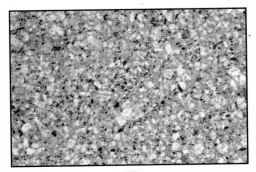

PEGMATITE

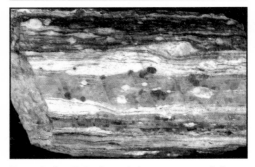

Pegmatite is a distinctive rock that can vary greatly in colour depending on its main constituents. Pegmatites form veins of rock and are usually found in association with large masses of granite. The most common type of pegmatite is granite pegmatite, which is made up mostly of the minerals feldspar and quartz. There may, however, be a great many other minerals present in varying proportions, such as mica, tourmaline, topaz, beryl, fluorite and garnet. Pegmatites are economically important as a source of many of these minerals. Pegmatite is a very coarse-grained rock and individual mineral crystals can be very large. Crystals of mica and quartz that are over three metres in length have been found.

DACITE

Dacite is the volcanic equivalent of granodiorite, being formed above the surface of the Earth from solidified lava rather than below it. Dacites are one of the most abundant rocks found around volcanic regions. The major mineral constituents of dacite are quartz and feldspar, along with small amounts of other minerals, such as hornblende. Dacite is generally a fine-grained rock although larger crystals may form against the finer background. Dacite forms a very slow-moving lava and the solid rock may still show banding formed when it was flowing. It may also be found as part of the debris from a volcanic eruption, ranging in size from large boulders to fine ash.

RHYOLITE

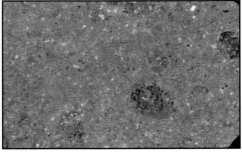

Rhyolite is the volcanic equivalent of granite, formed
above the ground from solidifying lava, rather than below
it. Rhyolite is generally glassy, or somewhat crystalline in
appearance and may have a resemblance to flint. It is
largely made up of quartz, feldspar and mica. Larger
crystals are often found set in the general background
of grains that are too fine to see with the naked eye. The
colour and texture of the rhyolite may show banding,
caused when the slow-moving lava from which the
rhyolite formed cooled rapidly. Rhyolites are also found
as volcanic fragments, formed when the lava has
erupted explosively from the volcano rather than flowing
out slowly.

OBSIDIAN

Obsidian is a black or greenish black glassy volcanic rock that is similar in its chemical constituents to granite, although very different in appearance. Reddish obsidian, which contains iron, is sometimes found. Obsidian is formed by the rapid cooling of a particular type of lava. The main component of obsidian is glass and it can give a very sharp edge when broken, a characteristic that was put to good use by early civilisations in Mexico and elsewhere for making tools. Snowflake obsidian, which is often polished as a decorative stone, has patches of white where the glass has become crystalised. Obsidian is often found in the same places as rhyolite.

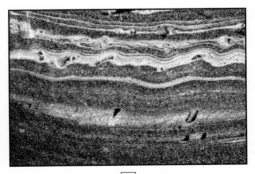

PITCHSTONE

Pitchstone is a form of volcanic glass, formed by the rapid cooling of a particular type of lava at or near the surface of the Earth. It is similar in composition to a wide range of other volcanic rocks. It is generally very dark in colour, but with a shiny surface rather like that of fresh tar. If there are iron rich minerals present, it may have a reddish colour. It is rather similar to obsidian but it contains more crystalline material than that rock. Small crystals of quartz and feldspar may be found embedded in the microscopically fine grains of the pitchstone. Pitchstone may have a banded or flow structure, a result of its rapid cooling and solidifying from the molten lava state.

PUMICE

Pumice is a pale grey, porous volcanic rock that is very light and full of numerous cavities. These cavities are formed by the frothing of gases dissolved in the lava from which the rock is formed as they expand and escape as the lava cools and solidifies. Pumice is rather like a hard sponge in texture and can often be light enough to float on water. It is frequently used as an abrasive and can be mixed with cement to form a lightweight building material. Because it is so light, pumice ejected from a volcano may be carried hundreds of kilometres away from the actual site of the eruption. Much of the debris that covered the town of Pompeii in AD79 was pumice.

DIORITE

Diorite is a medium to coarse-grained igneous rock that is formed deep within the Earth, usually in association with rocks such as granite and granodiorite. These rocks often form great masses called batholiths that form when magma from deep in the Earth swells up into the surrounding rocks. Batholiths are at the core of most major mountain ranges. Diorite is largely composed of light coloured feldspar and a variety of dark coloured minerals such as hornblende and mica, giving it a mottled grey and white appearance. Diorite may also contain a small proportion of quartz and rocks with a particularly high quartz content are often referred to as tonalite. Polished diorite is often used as a building stone.

ANDESITE

Andesite is the volcanic equivalent of diorite, forming at the surface through volcanic activity, rather than deep inside the Earth. A characteristic of andesite is its relatively light colour, which is a result of its high feldspar content. It is a fine grained or partly glassy rock, often with crystals of feldspar or hornblende set into the surface. Andesite erupts from volcanoes in places where one part of the Earth's surface is sliding beneath another. The Andes mountains of South America, for which andesite is named, are one such place. Andesite rocks are a common constituent of volcanic islands.

SYENITE

Syenite is a coarse-grained rock that is formed deep inside the Earth. It is a light coloured rock that can often be confused with granite and is in fact often associated with granite in its formation. The grains that make up syenite are generally of the same size but sometimes larger crystals will be found embedded with a background of smaller grains. The principal mineral component of syenite is alkali feldspar. Alkali feldspar syenite, which has a particularly high proportion of feldspar, is a particularly attractive rock with iridescent flecks of feldspar. Polished slabs of this decorative rock, which is also known as pale Labrador, are sometimes used as building stone.

TRACHYTE

Trachytes are the volcanic equivalent of syenites, being chemically similar but forming on the surface from cooling lava rather than deep inside the Earth's crust. Like other volcanic rocks, trachytes often reveal evidence in their structure of the fact that they once flowed. Like syenites they are rich in alkali feldspar. Trachytes can also occur as volcanic fragments when the material has been ejected explosively from the volcano rather than flowing. Trachytes are fine-grained rocks and generally light in colour, although darker minerals may also be present. Trachyte is often used for paving and flooring as it will not become shiny when rubbed.

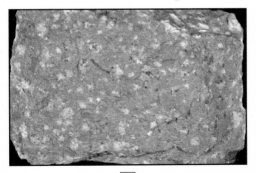

GABBRO

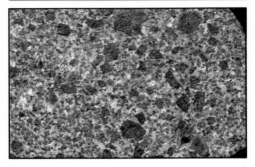

Gabbros are coarse-grained igneous rocks that form deep underground. There are several types of gabbro, divided according to the various proportions of the main constituents of the rock such as olivine and hornblende. One variety of gabbro is called troutstone because of its spotted appearance, caused by the minerals plagioclase and olivine. Layered gabbro, which has alternating layers of light and dark minerals, is also found. The layers can vary from a few centimetres to a metre or more in thickness and are caused by gravity settling out the light and dark components of the rock. It is a fragile rock but is sometimes used as a facing on buildings, particularly the more attractive dark gabbros.

BASALT

Basalt is the most abundant of all the volcanic rocks. It is made up primarily of feldspar and pyroxene. It is a dark-coloured, fine-grained rock that is generally black but may have a reddish or greenish crust. Basalt lavas are very fluid and can form huge sheets. It is the principal rock of the ocean floor, solidified from the lava that oozes out from the mid-ocean ridges, and of many oceanic islands, such as Mauna Loa, the chief island of Hawaii. Basalt sheets may break into regular columns as they cool, a phenomenon that can be seen in the Giant's Causeway in Northern Ireland. There are several different types of basalt, which vary according to their chemical composition.

PERIDOTITE

Peridotite is a coarse-grained dark and heavy igneous rock that forms deep inside the Earth. It is an uncommon rock at the surface. The most abundant minerals in peridotite are olivine and, usually, pyroxene. Peridotite usually forms when crystals of olivine settle out of molten basalt, forming a heavier layer at the bottom of the lighter basalt. From studies of the way earthquake waves move through the Earth, seismologists have concluded that the layer of the Earth immediately below the crust is very likely to be composed largely of peridotite. Peridotites are sometimes found mixed in with the basalts in areas of volcanic activity, having been brought to the surface by eruptions.

LAMPROPHYRE

Lamprophyres are actually a group of igneous rocks of varying compositions but characterised by dark coloured minerals with larger crystals embedded within a background of finer mineral crystals. Lamprophyres are usually found beside granites, diorites and syenites. They occasionally form as lavas, but more often they are formed underground in narrow dykes, when molten magma pours across layers of rock, or in sills, when the magma flows between layers of rock. Lamprophyres are chemically quite different from other igneous rocks, with higher concentrations of carbon dioxide, sulphur and other chemicals. The name comes from the Greek 'lampros', which means glistening.

GREISEN

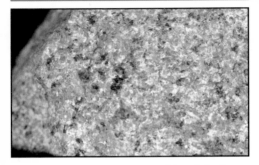

Greisen is a coarse-grained metamorphic rock that is formed from granite that has been acted upon by gases that are rich in fluorine. If fluorine vapours pass through the rock while it is still molten the feldspars in the granite are altered and become muscovite. Minerals rich in fluorine form in the granite and this produces a crumbly grey-white rock with a glittering appearance that is principally made up of quartz and muscovite, along with some topaz and fluorite as well. It can sometimes be seen forming veins a few centimetres across that gradually fade into the surrounding granite. Greisen is not a particularly common rock but it is sometimes important as a source of tin and tungsten.

SKARN

Skarn is a metamorphic rock with fine to medium-sized grains that is formed from limestone that contains other minerals as well. It is formed when molten magma flows into a limestone bed. Iron-, silicon- and magnesium-rich fluids in the magma react with the limestone and the impurities in it to form a variety of minerals that are rich in calcium, from the limestone, and silicon. Garnet and serpentine are typically among the minerals found in skarn. The different minerals may form a number of distinct patches in the rock, giving it a veined and banded appearance. Skarns often have deposits of metal ores, such as those containing copper and manganese.

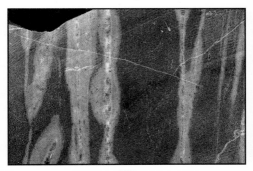

SPOTTED SLATE

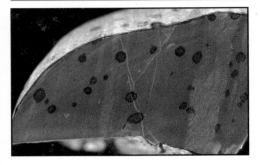

Spotted slate is a fine-grained black, purple or greenish-grey metamorphic rock with dark spots, which may often be indistinct. It is very similar to slate in its structure but does not have quite such a tendency to flake. Spotted slates are formed in the outer regions of aureoles, the zones where molten igneous rock intrudes into existing rock. The heat from the igneous rock changes ordinary slate or shale into spotted slate in this instance. Many of the minerals in the slate remain unaltered. Slate nearer to the igneous intrusion metamorphoses into hornfels. The dark irregular spots in the spotted slate are formed by the growth of minerals such as andalusite and cordierite.

HORNFELS

Hornfelses are hard, metamorphic rocks with fine to medium-sized grains with a granular texture and a variety of colours depending on the rock from which they were formed. Hornfelses often have a flinty appearance. They are formed in the heart of the aureoles where molten igneous rock meets other rock. Large mineral crystals, often of andalusite or garnet may be seen in the hornfels. The main mass of the rock is generally made up of quartz, feldspar and mica but hornfels can be very varied in their composition, depending on the source rock and the temperature to which it was heated. Hornfelses are frequently found blending into spotted slates and slates.

MARBLE

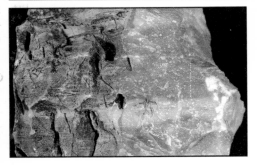

Marble is a crystalline metamorphic rock that is formed by the transformation of limestone. It is a relatively soft rock and easily scratched with a penknife. Some types of marble have a granular, sugary surface. Pure marble, like that found in Carrara, Italy, is almost entirely white and is much prized for sculptures. It is the various impurities that may be found in it that give marble the colours and patterns often seen. For example, traces of iron and magnesium produce green minerals such as olivine and sometimes yellow-brown garnet. Marble takes a polish very well and it is a popular stone for decorating buildings. The Taj Mahal is mainly constructed from white marble.

QUARTZITE

As the name might suggest, quartzite is composed mainly of quartz and it is formed from sandstone that has recrystallised under great heat and pressure. It is a medium-grained rock, which may be white, grey or reddish in colour, and somewhat similar in appearance to marble. However, it can be readily distinguished from marble because it has a much harder surface. The grains of quartzite are firmly bound together and the rock will break across the grains. Small flakes of mica may be present between the grains of quartzite if there have been clay impurities in the original sandstone. Quartzite is sometimes used in buildings for flooring.

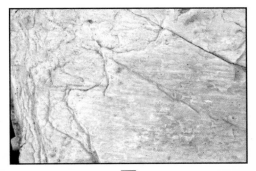

SLATE

Slate is a fine-grained, brittle metamorphic rock that will split easily into thin slabs. This splitting is due to the minerals in the slate being aligned in parallel. Slate is the metamorphic equivalent of shale. Slates are mostly made up of the minerals white mica, chlorite, quartz, feldspar and graphite, but the individual grains of each mineral are far too small to be distinguished by the naked eye. The example above has crystals of pyrites embedded in it. Slates can be found in a variety of colours – slate from Ballachulish in Scotland is black, while the slate from Skiddaw in the Lake District is greeny purple. Slate has been widely used as a roofing material in the past although it has now been largely superseded.

PHYLLITE

Phyllite is a greyish-green metamorphic rock that is an intermediate between slate and schist. It is formed in the same way as slate, from clays or shales, but the mineral crystals formed are slightly larger, giving the rock a coarser texture. Phyllite can be distinguished from slate by the sheen of mica crystals that can be seen on a fractured surface. Like slate, phyllite will split easily into slabs along a plane. Again, this is due to the parallel alignment of the grains that make up the rock. Occasionally phyllite may have tiny crystals of garnet visible, set into the surrounding minerals. Schist has bigger grains than phyllite.

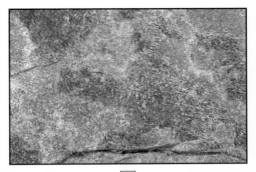

MICA SCHIST

Mica schist is a medium to coarse-grained metamorphic rock that is formed from sedimentary rocks under great temperature and pressure. There are actually several different types of schist, with the main minerals found in all of them being chlorite, biotite and muscovite. The colours of the schists depend on the proportions of the minerals present. Those with a high proportion of chlorite are bottle green in colour, schists with a lot of biotite are dark brown or black. Mica schists (most are rich in mica) will have a sparkle from the mica. There may be folds visible in the rock. Parts of the rock flake off very easily, a property known as schistosity, which is due to the alignment in parallel of the crystals.

GNEISS

Gneiss (pronounced 'nice') is a coarse-grained metamorphic rock that is formed under conditions of increasing temperature and pressure, deep inside the Earth's crust. Gneisses are often highly folded. They frequently occur in association with granites and schists. The structure of gneiss is similar to that of schist, with thin bands of mica alternating with lighter coloured granular bands of quartz and feldspar. Garnets are frequently found in gneiss. Paragneisses are formed from sedimentary rocks and orthogneisses are formed from igneous rocks. Gneiss over 3700 million years old was found by geologists near Amitsoq, Greenland.

MIGMATITES

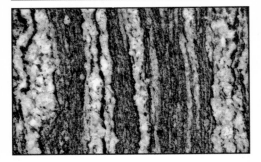

Migmatites are coarse-grained rocks that are thought to to have been formed by a combination of metamorphic and igneous process. Their formation occurs deep enough inside the Earth's crust for melting of the rocks to occur. If a gneiss is completely melted and recrystallises, a rock similar in appearance and composition to granite will be produced. Migmatites represent intermediate stages in this process, varying according to how much of the original rock was melted so that they are combinations of granite-like and gneiss-like rocks. Migmatites have a granular texture and frequently have banding of dark and light coloured mineral components, like gneiss. They may also be formed from schists.

AMPHIBOLITE

Amphibolites are generally formed by the metamorphosis of igneous rocks, such as basalt lavas and dolerite. They are green to dark green or black in colour, sometimes speckled with white or grey, and medium to coarse-grained in texture. The rock may show a distinct layered structure, although it does not split very readily. Larger crystals of minerals such as garnets are often found growing in crevices in the rock. Banding of alternate light and dark layers may be present in some samples. Amphibolites are fairly massive rocks and folding is rare. The major mineral present in amphibolite is hornblende.

GARNET SCHIST

Garnet schist is a metamorphosed form of sedimentary rock such as mudstone, which, as the name would suggest, contains well defined crystals of garnet that can measure around 5mm in diameter. It forms in regions where rocks have been deeply buried, so pressure is high, but the temperature is also relatively low. Such conditions are found along the edges of continental plates where ocean crust is being pulled down beneath continental crust. Garnet schist is a medium to coarse-grained rock. It has a layered structure, due to the alignment of mica crystals within the rock. The mica can give the rock a glittering appearance. Small folds may sometimes be seen in the rock.

ECLOGITE

Eclogites are attractive medium to large-grained rocks that contain red garnet and bright green pyroxene. Other minerals present may include hornblende, quartz, mica, dolomite and others. Eclogites are found as small bodies in association with migmatites and in bands in schist formations. Eclogites are chemically similar to basalt but are slightly more dense, a consequence of their formation at high pressures and temperatures deep within the Earth's crust. The exact means of their formation is not known, but many geologists consider them to be igneous rocks, possibly dolerites, that have undergone intense metamorphism.

SERPENTINITE

Serpentinite is composed almost entirely of serpentine minerals, although hornblende, mica and garnet can also be present. It is a coarse to medium-grained, soft and compact metamorphic rock that is pale green to greenish black in colour and may also have green and red streaks and blotches. Weathered rock can have a dull waxy appearance. Most of the crystals that make up serpentinite can be readily discerned with the naked eye. Serpentine bands are often visible running through the rock. Serpentine is formed when peridotite is altered by the addition of water. Serpentinite is typically found in folded metamorphic rocks, and may also occur in massive outcrops.

CONGLOMERATES

Conglomerates are coarse-grained rocks that are made up of rounded rock fragments over 2mm in diameter. These larger fragments are bound together by fine-grained material or cement. Conglomerates are highly variable with regard to colour as this is dependent on the types of pebbles present and their relative proportions. The larger pebbles in the conglomerate are usually river gravel or beach shingle, the most common rocks being quartzite, flint, chert and a variety of igneous rocks. In some conglomerates, an example being Hertfordshire Puddingstone, the surrounding cement is just as hard as the flint pebbles embedded within it.

BRECCIAS

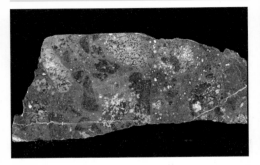

Breccias are coarse-grained rocks, similar in structure to conglomerates, but differing from them in that the large fragments set in the fine- to medium-grained cement are unworn and angular. Breccia can be practically any colour as it can contain any rock type and any mixture of types. Some of the fragments in breccia will have been formed by landslides, others by the collapse of limestone caves. Spaces between the rock fragments are filled with finer rock waste and this eventually cements the larger fragments together to form the breccia. Fault breccia is formed where rocks are shattered and fragmented when there is movement along a geological faultline.

TILL & TILLITES

Till, also known as boulder clay, is the deposit of clay, mud, gravel and boulders left behind by a retreating glacier.All sizes of fragments are mixed up together in till, ranging from ones no bigger than sandgrains to boulders weighing several tonnes, bound together in a clay or sandy matrix. Tillites are formed when the matter that makes up the till are consolidated over time and form hard rock. The sandy matrix may become shale or even slate. The till left by the last ice age was deposited far too recently for tillite to form. However, the discovery of fossils in tillites has allowed geologists to determine that there have been several ice ages in the Earth's past.

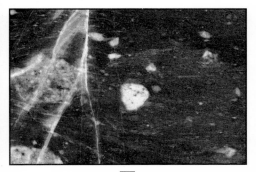

QUARTZ ARENITES

Quartz arenites are a type of the medium-grained sedimentary rock more commonly called sandstone. Over 95% of the rock is composed of quartz grains, its strength determined by the composition of the cement holding the grains together. Some sandstones are formed by the depositing of rock fragments in water, usually in shallow seas, whereas others are formed from sand deposited n desert environments. Wind blown grains can be recognised by the frosted appearance of the surface. Fossils are commonly found in sandstones. If the sandstone is particularly porous, deposits of oil or natural gas may be formed within it. Sandstone is important in the manufacture of glass and is also used in construction.

LITHIC ARENITES

Lithic arenites are sandstones in which quartz forms a
lower proportion of the composition of the rock than
it does in quartz arenites. It is still by far the major
component, however, making up about three quarters
of the mass of the rock. The other grains in the rock may
be derived from any rock capable of being eroded into
sandgrain-sized particles. Many of the sandstones found
around the world are in fact lithic arenites. The colour of
these sandstones is very variable. The texture is generally
medium-grained although a fair range of fragment sizes
may be observed. Fossils are frequently discovered in
lithic arenites as they are in other sandstones.

ARKOSES

Arkoses are a type of sandstone that is rich in the mineral feldspar, which may form up to a third of the mass of the rock. If granite is rapidly weathered, as may happen in desert and semi-desert conditions, feldspars are released and deposited, eventually forming arkoses. The sediment must be deposited rapidly to prevent the feldspar from decomposing and forming clays. The grains of feldspar are often angular rather than rounded and this can give the arkoses a gritty feel. They are medium grained, verging on coarse grained. Arkoses are usually grey, pink or red in colour, the red and pink colour coming from the feldspar. Fossils are rarely found in arkoses.

GREYWACKES

Greywackes are another type of sandstone in which the fine-grained matrix holding the fragments together may comprise 15% or more of the rock. They are dark, hard rocks, ranging from grey to black in colour, sometimes with a greenish tinge when chlorite is present. The fragments held in the matrix are coarse to medium grained and generally poorly sorted. The larger grains may be either rounded or angular. In addition to quartz, the fragments in the rock may consist of feldspar, micas, small pieces of other rocks and minerals such as hornblende. The matrix generally consists of clay minerals such as the green chlorite. Fossils are very rare.

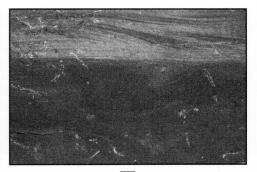

SILTSTONES

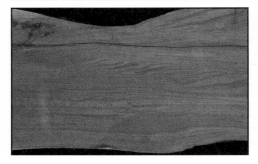

Siltstones are intermediate rocks, between sandstones and shales. They are fine-grained sedimentary rocks in which the size of the grains varies from the just visible to the microscopically small. Siltstone beds are often found alongside shales and sandstones. Siltstones have a slightly gritty feel. Mica is usually found in fairly large proportions in siltstone, and it may be seen sparkling in the rock, along with quartz and feldspar and some other minerals. Siltstones are formed from grains of silt deposited along slow-moving rivers and in lakes. It may also form on the sea bed some distance out from the shore. Fossils are often found in large quantities in siltstones.

MUDSTONE

Mudstone, as its name implies, is a sedimentary rock that has been formed from mud or clay that has been compressed and recrystallised. It forms in places such as oceans and lakes where mud has been deposited. It is a very fine-grained rock, the grains too small to be seen with the naked eye. Mudstone can be very varied in colour, ranging from grey, green and blue to red. It is composed of a mixture of clay minerals, together with some quartz, feldspar and mica. The fragments are arranged at random throughout the rock and mudstone will break up into rough lumps. It is similar to shale in some of its characteristics and often contains fossils

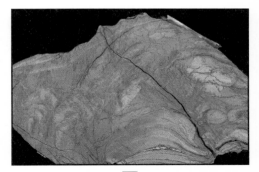

FOSSILIFEROUS LIMESTONE

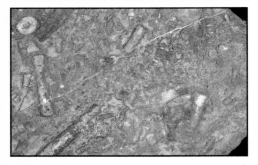

Limestones are sedimentary rocks that are composed mainly of calcites with a proportion of quartz clay and other minerals. The calcite may often be derived from fossil shells and coral. Fossiliferous limestone consists of a number of fossils held together by a calcite cement. The texture of the rock depends on the fossils in it and ranges from a fine-grained, almost porcelain-like texture to a coarse-grained one. The colour is also variable, ranging from white to red, brown or black. Different types of limestone are distinguished by the types of fossils held in the matrix. For example, pelagic limestones, which form in deep water, are made up of the remains of floating organisms, such as plankton.

CHALK

Chalk is a pure form of limestone, almost entirely formed of calcite, that is usually found in thick beds. It is a very soft rock, white or light grey in colour. It is made up of the remains of living organisms; mostly microscopic plates from algae called coccoliths and minute shells from other creatures called formanifera. Most chalk beds were formed during the Cretaceous period, between 140 and 65 million years ago, probably deposited in quiet seas at considerable depth where there was no wave disturbance. The Cretaceous takes its name from the Latin for chalk, creta. Modern blackboard chalk is in fact made from gypsum, which is less dusty than real chalk.

DOLOMITE

Dolomites, also sometimes known as magnesian limestone, are a type of limestone rock where some of the calcite has been replaced by the mineral dolomite. Dolomites are grey, brown or reddish in colour and have an even, crystalline texture. They are usually darker than other limestones. Fewer fossils are found in dolomites than in other limestones. This may in part be due to the recrystallisation that takes place as the original calcite limestone is replaced by dolomite. Often patches of unaltered limestone are found in the dolomite, sometimes as spheres of calcite surrounded by softer dolomite. The Houses of Parliament in London were built from dolomitic limestone.

IRONSTONES

Ironstones are a group of sedimentary rocks which, as the name would suggest, are rich in iron, which makes up at least 15% of the rock. The presence of the iron gives them their characteristic rusty-red appearance when the rock is weathered. Some geologists prefer to call these rock bands iron formations rather than ironstones because of their composition and the way in which they form can vary so widely. They are often found between beds of limestones and sandstones and are frequently rich in fossils. The cement holding the grains together is often made of calcite or dolomite. Ironstones are of great economic importance, obviously as a source of the metal.

CHERTS & FLINTS

Cherts and flints are a form of fine-grained sedimentary crystalline silica known as chalcedony. Usually nowadays the two are distinguished. Chert and flint form rounded nodules that can be widely different in form. The nodules are usually blue-grey to black in colour, but weathered stone can have a white, powdery crust. Chert nodules, such as the one shown here, are found most often in limestones and it can also be found in massive, although quite thin beds. Nodules of flint, which are frequently found embedded in chalk beds, are sometimes hollow and a fossil may be found inside. Flint can be broken to give a sharp edge and was commonly used during the Stone Age to make tools and weapons.

STONY IRON

Stony iron meteorites are composed of around 50% silica and 50% nickel-iron alloy. Many of the silicate minerals are similar to the types found on Earth, including olivine, pyroxene and feldspar. Stony iron meteorites are rare, making up no more than 4% of the meteorites that fall to Earth. They are rock-like in appearance and the surface is frequently rough and pitted with some of the silicate minerals removed by weathering, if the stone is old. Evidence of the meteorite's fiery passage through the atmosphere may also be seen. A meteorite that has recently fallen to Earth will have a black fusion crust caused by the melting of the outer layers due to friction.

TEKTITE

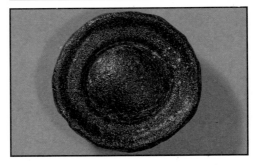

Tektites are small silicon-rich glassy objects that were once thought to be meteorites but are now thought to have originated on Earth. They are found only in a few regions, principally South Australia. Their composition is not unlike that of many volcanic rocks. Most are small, the majority being between 1 and 3cm across. They are varied in shape, with button-shaped, disc-shaped, spherical and teardrop-shaped examples being found. Most are jet black in colour, although some are dark green. Thin flakes of the tektites may be transparent. A current theory is that tektites were formed by the melting of the surrounding rock by the impact of a meteor.

CHONDRITE

Chondrites form the largest group of meteorites that strike the Earth's surface. They contain small, spherical grains of olivine or pyroxene called chondrules along with nickel-iron alloy and other minerals. Chondrites are generally rounded or dome-shaped, sharp-edged specimens being those that have shattered on impact. The fusion crust formed by frictional heating as the chondrite passes through the atmosphere tends to be thicker on chondrites than on stony iron meteorites. The interior of the stone is usually grey or dark grey in colour. Chondrites have been around since the solar system was formed and specimens have been dated at 4,600 million years old.

PLANT FOSSIL: LEPIDODENDRON

Lepidodendron is an example of a Coal Measure plant that lived between 345 and 270 million years ago. The Coal Measures are the major source of fossil plants. Lepidodendron has been found in various places around the world, including Europe, North Africa and China and was almost certainly one of the principal plants of the period. It would normally reach a height of about 30 metres (100ft), although some specimens probably topped 50 metres (160ft), with roots stretching another 12 metres (40ft) below the surface. The photograph shown here shows a section of the trunk. Some 110 different species of Lepidodendron have been identified. There are no living examples of Lepidodendron today.

PLANT FOSSIL: ANNULARIA

Annularia are members of a group of plants that were common in the Carboniferous period and are represented today by the horsetails. Some had trunks 30 metres (100ft) tall before the branches were reached. A typical feature of Annularia fossils (shown in the photograph here) is the way in which the leaves are arranged radially around the stem, seemingly in one plane. This may be due to the fossilisation process having flattened them out but it has also been suggested that this in fact was how the plant appeared in life, with the leaves spread to obtain maximum exposure to sunlight. The length of the leaves varies, some specimens reaching 8cm (3in).

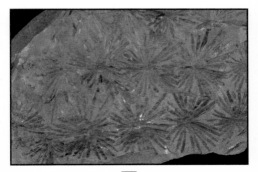

PLANT FOSSIL: PECOPTERIS

Pecopteris is a fern-like plant from the Carboniferous period, around 390 million years ago. It may well in fact be a true fern rather than one of the ancestors of ferns. Other species of fern-like plants produced seeds, rather than the spores produced by true ferns. Pecopteris has a number of small leaflets, which can be seen in the photograph shown here. The leaflets had a distinct mid-rib and were attached to the stem by the whole base rather than by a leaf stalk. Pecopteris is one of the Coal Measure plants, the remains of which formed the coal reserves we have used for fuel, and specimens are often found in coal seams. Tip heaps from mines are a good place to find Coal Measure specimens.

PLANT FOSSIL: BENNETITALES

This group of plants was an important part of the
flora in Jurassic times, 195 to 140 million years ago.
They had worldwide distribution and were among the
first plants to have a reproductive structure that is
similar to that of modern day flowers. The leaves of
Bennetitales are fern-like with the leaves attached to
the wide main stem. A typical 'flower' would have a
broad, disc-likebase from which large petal-like
stamens would curve outwards and inwards.The
photograph here shows a leaf specimen from
Pterophyllum, one of the Bennetitales, where the fern-
like structure of the leaves can be seen.

PLANT FOSSIL: LAURUS

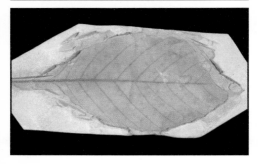

The leaf shown here is from a member of the Angiosperms, or flowering plants, the most advanced plant group, which first appeared around 140 million years ago and is now the most successful plant group on Earth. They are distinguished from other plants by their flowers and the fact that their seeds are protected within pods, which also provide nutrients for germination. This is a leaf from a Laurus species, which resembles a modern-day laurel tree. This was a very important family in Cretaceous times. As can be seen, the leaves were undivided and the veins are quite distinct, with secondary veins branching from a central, main vein.

FOSSIL WOOD

This is an example of fossil wood, which is very common in many parts of the world, being most frequently encountered in arid or desert areas It is possible to produce attractive specimens by cutting and polishing fossil wood, although specialised equipment is required for this. Sections are frequently offered for sale for their curiosity and decorative value. The photograph shows a typical cross section of wood from a dicotyledon, one of the flowering plants. This is possibly a Quercus species, one of the ancestors of present-day oak trees. The growth rings in the wood are very clearly visible.

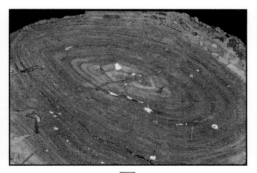

CORAL: HEXAGONARIA

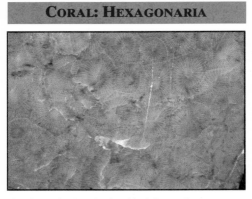

Corals are simple animals, with skeletons that are composed of calcite. They are frequently preserved as fossils. Many corals are solitary and single specimens leave small fossil remains. Others, however, such as the Hexagonaria species shown in the photograph are colonial and, consequently, leave much more visible remains. A single coral is called a corallite. Hexagonaria was found throughout the world during the Devonian period 395 to 345 million years ago and formed massive colonies. The individual corallites are separated by strong walls. Strong horizontal wrinkles and vertical grooves are distinctly visible.

CORAL: HALYSITES

Halysites are an example of corals that lived betwen 500 and 400 million years ago. Specimens have been found from around the world. It is an example of a colonial coral. The individual corallites are elongated, growing more or less in parallel, and joined together along whole adjoining edges, so that the colony forms distinctive chain-like patterns as can be seen in the photograph below. In cross-section the individual corallites are circular. Only two other forms of Halysites have been discovered, both dating from the same period but restricted to North America. They differ slightly in the cross-sectional shape of the corallites.

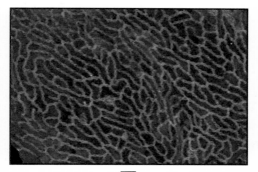

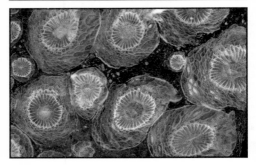

Lonsdaleia is a member of the group of corals known as the Rugosa. These first appeared during the Paleozoic period, and can be found either as solitary specimens or forming colonies. The individual corallites may be slightly separated from each other, although they are just as often found in close contact. Strongly defined walls mark the boundaries between each of the corallites. Vertical divisions within each corallite, called septa, are long and there is a central pit on the upper surface. Lonsdaleia is somewhat similar to Hexagonaria, shown on page 66, in its overall appearance, but cross sections through the corallites will reveal their different internal structures.

CORAL: THECOSMILIA

Thecosmilia is a colonial coral that was found in warm, shallow seas throughout the world, from the Triassic to the Cretaceous periods. It had particularly large corallites, which were cylindrical or like squat cones in shape with a circular appearance in cross-section. The dividing septa within each corallite were very numerous and had serrated upper edges. The septa are clearly visible on the outer surface of a good specimen. In fact, the septa may extend above the upper surface of the corallite and can appear to overlap on the upper face of the specimen. Horizontal divisions, called tabulae, may also be seen near the centre of the corallite.

SPONGE: PERONIDELLA

Sponges are the simplest forms of multi-cellular animals. They have no nervous system and no internal organs. The skeleton, which is rich in calcium or silicon-containing minerals, will be fossilised under the right conditions. Sponges are one of the earliest multi-cellular lifeforms to have evolved, dating back to the Precambrian period. They are marine creatures, living either singly or in colonies. Adult sponges live attached to the sea floor or to the back of larger marine creatures. Peronidella was common in the seas during the Triassic and Cretaceous periods. It is a medium-sized sponge with a number of cylinders radiating out from a common base.

BRYOZOAN: FENESTELLA

The Bryozoans are aquatic animals that form moss-like colonies in both salt and fresh water. Each individual in the colony lives in a tube called a zooecium and the colony is called a zoarium. The zooecium is formed from calcium compounds secreted by the bryozoan and it is this which fossilises. They are somewhat similar to jellyfish and sea anemones but their body structure is much more complex. Bryozoan fossils are known from as early as the Ordovician period. Fenestella, shown here, formed a net-like colony, spread out in a fan shape. The tubes of the zooecium are generally fairly short. Paired rows of pores can be made out on the upper surface.

The Membranipora species are part of a group of
bryozoans called the Cheilostomata, which includes the
commonest living species of bryozoan. These are fairly
recent fossils, dating back only as far as the Miocene,
between 5 and 23 million years ago. Membranipora is
one of the commonest bryozoan fossils found in chalk.
The zooecia are arranged in regular rows in this
specimen, although the whole colony may take up an
irregular shape. The opening of each zooecium can show
wide variety in their shapes. The colony tends to encrust
a rock surface or the back of a larger water creature,
such as a sea urchin.

Molluscs are one of the most important fossil groups. Their calcium-containing shells fossilise readily and they are often used to date the rocks in which they are found. Gastropods, or snails, are one of the major mollusc groups. Bellerophon fossils have been found worldwide and it was probably fairly common during the Silurian and Triassic periods. It has a wide shell, sometimes up to 8 centimetres across, that flares near the opening. The last whorl, or complete coil of the shell, covers the previous whorls, which are visible in deep holes on either side of the shell. A prominent ridge can be seen around the middle of the whorl and there are also growth lines.

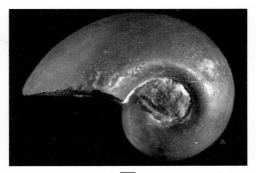

GASTROPOD: TURRITELLA

Turritella is a type of gastropod that first appeared in the Cretaceous period around 80 million years ago. Examples of living species can still be found in the seas today. Fossil Turritella have been found throughout the world. They were herbivorous animals that lived on soft sea floors. The shell of Turritella is long and conical in shape, with large numbers of spirally arranged marks around the curving whorls. Very thin growth marks can be distinguished on the shell of a good specimen. Turitella grew typically to around 4 centimetres in length. The opening at the bottom of the shell is generally oval in shape.

GASTROPOD: POLEUMITA

Poleumita is a fairly large gastropod that lived during the Silurian period between 430 and 400 million years ago. Fossil specimens of this snail have been unearthed in rocks in North America and in Europe. A good-sized specimen would be about 7 centimetres in diameter, although some have been found that are 9 centimetres wide. There are slightly raised spines on the shoulder, which will be seen easily in a good specimen and the shell is ornamented by fine lines radiating out from the main whorl. The aperture of the shell is a distinctive shape, being rather like a parallelogram notched in the upper left corner and curved in the lower left corner.

Parallelodon is one of the bivalve molluscs, a class to which the present-day oysters, cockles and clams belong. The earliest bivalves appear in rocks dating back to the Cambrian period and from that time they have spread out and diversified. Parallelodon was widespread during the Devonian and Jurassic periods, fossil examples of these molluscs have been found worldwide. The shell is somewhat elongated in appearance, with a long back section and a shortened front end. Projections of the shell called hinge teeth can be seen near the front end of the hinge, which forms a straight line down the shell. The teeth are short and curving.

AMMONITE: GASTRIOCERAS

Gastrioceras is a member of an extinct group of animals called ammonites. Related to present-day octopus and cuttlefish, the ammonites first appeared during the Devonian period and then disappeared from the fossil record after the Cretaceous period. They have a spiral shell, made up of numerous gas-filled chambers, the last of which contained the living animal. Ammonites ranged widely in size, a large specimen reaching perhaps two metres across, with the smallest being coin-sized. In the course of evolution, ammonite shells became increasingly complex. Gastrioceras was widespread during the Carboniferous period.

AMMONITE: DACTYLIOCERAS

Dactylioceras was one of the commonest ammonites of the Jurassic period. Examples have been found throughout the world and it is particularly abundant in European rocks. It is a medium-sized ammonite growing to between 5 and 10 centimetres in diameter. It has an attractively ornamented shell with a number of clearly defined, closely packed ribs, denser towards the centre of the whorl, radiating out from the central spiral. During the Middle Ages in Yorkshire, people used to carve eyes and mouths on to ammonite fossils and then claim that they were snakes that had been turned to stone by St Hilda.

GRAPTOLITE: DIPLOGRAPTUS

The graptolites were a group of tiny colonial animals that were common from the Cambrian to the Carboniferous periods, but are now extinct. Each colony would form a number of branch-like structures called stipes. Each individual in the colony was housed in a cup-like structure called a theca. Graptolites changed rapidly during the course of their evolution, and this makes them valuable as a means of dating the rocks in which they are found. Diplograptus was important during the Ordovician and Silurian periods. The individual thecae are arranged on each side of the stipes, giving them a serrated appearance.

ECHINODERM: PENTACRINITES

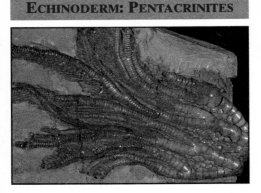

Pentacrinites was a member of the echinoderms, a group of marine animals that first appeared in the seas of the Cambrian era and are still widespread today. Starfish, sea urchins and sea cucumbers are modern-day examples. Pentacrinites is a sea lily, a type of echinoderm that could grow to a considerable size, with a stem perhaps a metre long carrying numerous long, branching arms. In cross-section the stem resembles a five-pointed star. Hair-like cirri may sometimes be seen on the stem. Pentacrinites was common during the Mesozoic period and fossil specimens have been found in North America and Europe.

TRILOBITE: BUMASTUS

Trilobites are the most commonly found fossil arthropods, the family of animals that includes spiders, insects and crustaceans. Trilobites first appeared during the Cambrian period, becoming extinct in the Permian. Bumastus is a type of trilobite that was found worldwide during the Ordovician and Silurian periods. It had a rather long drawn out appearance with the head and tail region being roughly similar in size. The head was rounded with large swellings on either side. The central 'spine' or axis, is not as clearly defined as it is in some trilobites. The thorax is divided into eight to ten clearly defined segments. The smooth tail is convex in shape.

TRILOBITE: ENCRINURUS

Encrinurus is a type of trilobite that was distributed worldwide in the seas and oceans of the Ordovician to Silurian periods. It is quite a handsome specimen with a head that is distinctly larger than the tail. The glabella, the central section of the head, widens towards the front of the animal. The eyes, situated on either side of the glabella, are rather pronounced. There are small spines, called genal spines, on the side of the head. Encrinurus' thorax is divided into eleven or twelve well defined segments divided by grooves, while the tail divides into a further four or five segments. The shell is strongly ornamented.

TRILOBITE: PHACOPS

Phacops was a type of trilobite that was found worldwide in the seas of the Devonian to Silurian periods. The specimen shown here is typical of the Phacops species that have been found in North America. The head was larger than the tail and was characterised by a narrow central region widening towards the front. The head of many specimens is decorated by a number of raised protuberances. The eyes were large and conspicuous and are often well preserved in fossil specimens. The thorax was divided into around 11 segments and the back edge of Phacops was rounded and smooth. In common with other trilobites, Phacops could roll into a ball.

TRILOBITE: PARADOXIDES

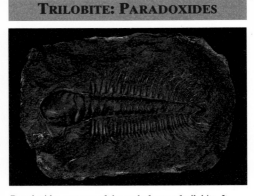

Paradoxides was one of the early forms of trilobite. It lived during the middle part of the Cambrian period, from around 550 to 530 million years ago. It has been found in North America, Europe and Australia. It was fairly big for a trilobite, growing to around 20 centimetres in length. The head, or cephalon, has a pair of spines at the rear which are long and backward curving. The thorax is divided into between 16 and 21 segments, each of which has a pair of backward pointing spines. These spines increase in size towards the rear of the animal, the final two stretching back over the tail. The tail is small with a straight back edge.

SHARK TOOTH

The skeleton of a shark, being composed of soft cartilage rather than bone, rarely fossilizes. The teeth, which are much harder, are found most often in rocks dating from around 2 to 140 million years ago. Many specimens, such as the one shown here, are triangular and pointed with serrated edges. A shark armed with such teeth was probably a large predator similar to the present great white shark. The fact that sharks are still around today marks them out, with crocodiles, as one of the most successful of animals. A comparison of fossil shark teeth with those from living specimens helped to demonstrate that fossils were the remains of once living things.

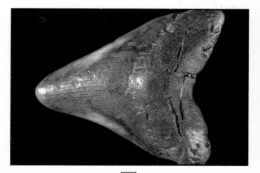

CROCODILE SKULL

Reptiles were the most important of the world's large animals from around 340 to 140 million years ago. Among their number were the best-known prehistoric animals of all – the dinosaurs. Crocodiles are among the most common of the fossil reptiles and the fact that there are still several species around today is evidence of their continuing success. A cast of a nearly complete crocodile skull is shown here. Large fossil remains such as this are found only rarely and you would be very lucky indeed to unearth such a aspecimen. Crocodile teeth can vary in shape, even in a single ndividual. The sharply pointed upper crowns are usually black, with long, lighter coloured roots.

BEAR TOOTH

Mammals first appeared at the time of the dinosaurs. Their remains are most common in deposits dating back to the Pleistocene, about two million years ago, and may be abundant in much earlier deposits in some locations. Most mammal remains are identified by examination of the teeth, particularly the cheek teeth. The example shown here is a bear's tooth, one of the big canines, or fangs. These are large teeth, with swollen roots. A bear's cheek teeth have low crowns, with rounded cusps and other swellings and grooves. The cheek teeth of some pigs are somewhat similar. Flesh-eating mammals such as cats have cheek teeth with sharp flesh-slicing edges.

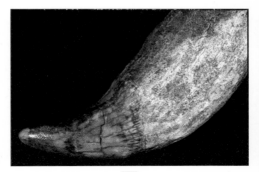

GEOLOGICAL TIMELINE

Quaternary

A period of geological time that is still in progress. It is divided into:

Holocene: began 10,000 years ago, from the end of the last ice age to the present day.

Pleistocene: 1.64 million to 10,000 years ago; humans evolve into modern *Homo sapiens* in this epoch.

Tertiary

The period during which the mammals took over the ecological gaps left by the extinction of the dinosaurs and became the dominant land animals. The continents took on their present positions during the

Tertiary period. It is divided into:

Pliocene: 5.2 to 1.64 million years ago; humanoid apes evolve in Africa.

Miocene: 23.5 to 5.2 million years ago; grasslands spread across the continents and hooved mammals evolve.

Oligocene: 35.5 to 23.5 million years ago.

Eocene: 56.5 to 35.5 million years ago.

Palaeocene: 65 to 56.5 million years ago; mammals begin to spread out and diversify following the disappearance of the dinosaurs and other great reptiles.

Cretaceous

146 to 65 million years ago; flowering plants evolve, the dinosaurs have their heyday; a typical rock of the Cretaceous period is chalk.

Jurassic

208 to 146 million years ago; birds evolve, along with many species of dinosaurs, great forests of ferns and conifers grow up, typical rocks of the Jurassic period are limestones and iron ores.

Triassic

245 to 208 million years ago; early dinosaurs and other reptiles start to evolve, and the first mammals also begin to appear in the late Triassic, a typical rock of the Triassic period is sandstone.

Permian

290 to 245 million years ago; amphibians and reptiles flourish, cone-bearing plants evolve, extensive deserts, many corals and forms of marine life become extinct, typical rocks are limestones and sandstones.

Carboniferous

363 to 290 million years ago; amphibians are plentiful, reptiles evolve, typical rocks are limestones and coal deposits, formed from the remains of swamp plants.

Devonian

408 to 360 million years ago; first land plants appear, amphibians evolve from air-breathing fish, first insects appear, typical rocks are desert sandstones.

Silurian

439 to 409 million years ago; many armoured jawless fish in the oceans, first fish with jaws appear, first land plants appear, coral-like animals form huge reefs, typical rocks are shale and limestone.

Ordovician

510 to 439 million years ago; animal life is confined to the seas, first fish evolve, typical rocks from this period are mudstones and shale.

Cambrian

570 to 510 million years ago; many animal groups appear including marine animals with hard outer shells, such as trilobites, leaving many fossils, typical rocks are shale, slate and sandstone.

Precambrian

from the formation of the Earth 4.6 billion years ago to 570 million years ago; it is divided into:

Proterozoic: roughly 3.5 billion to 570 million years ago, the time during which simple lifeforms first appeared.

Archaean: from the formation of the Eart to around 3.5 billion years ago, the period before life existed on Earth.

TITLES IN THIS SERIES INCLUDE: